Disclaimer

The content of this book is not sponsored by, affiliated with or endorsed by any company or government agency mentioned herein. Any references to specific products or services or details are for informational and/or educational purposes only and do not constitute an endorsement or recommendation.

The primary aim of this book is to highlight the dedication and determination of individuals around the world who are navigating the legal immigration process and adhering to U.S. immigration laws. It will also hopefully shed light on the extreme dangers of a government encouraging the dangerous unnecessary and illegal migration of millions of unvetted individuals and the extreme harm this practice causes to women and children who are many times forced into human trafficking. These practices are also pushing a country to the brink of disaster, dividing a wonderful nation that is supposed to be a beacon for the rest of the world and humanity to emulate.

It is not intended to diminish or disrespect anyone from any country across the globe.

Presenting the facts as we interpret them, based on our observations of the world around us.

Published in the United States of America, 2024
Cover design by Josh Bannister
Cover art by Ethel Ocaña
All rights reserved.
Library of Congress Control Number: 2024925547

Photograph 2013 by Ethel Ocaña

Ethel on tarmac with her nephew waiting to board the U.S. Air Force
C-130 Hercules cargo plane.
Daniel Romualdez Airport Tacloban City
Nov 2013

Introduction

America is a land of immigrants. The journey to the land of the free has not always been easy, though, even for people who follow the rules. Here we tell the true short story of Ethel, a middle-aged woman from a rural province in Philippines who overcame an unbelievable series of challenges, each one more daunting and stressful than the last. After surviving one of the deadliest typhoons in Philippine history to navigating the complexities of the U.S. immigration system, Ethel has experienced perseverance, heartbreak, and hope.

Ethel is a fully credentialed registered nurse who desired to contribute to the healthcare system in a country in need of medical professionals. Her dream of migrating "legally" to the United States was met with overwhelming frustration. Despite passing the USRN NCLEX exam, the first step required, once she began her journey navigating the complicated labyrinth of the U.S. immigration system, Ethel found herself caught in an unending bureaucratic nightmare. Her journey, as of today, is not yet done.

The U.S. immigration system is overrun by the millions of undocumented migrants illegally crossing the U.S. southern border every year. Because of this, Ethel's application is repeatedly delayed and put on the back burner as the U.S. apparently prioritizes handling the surge of illegal migrants. Ethel is in a waiting game and uncertain of when or even if she will ever be able to legally migrate to the country that holds the key to her future.

Ethel's story is not just about her personal journey, but also a reflection of the larger struggle faced by well educated vetted and medically-qualified professionals from around the world who seek to legally migrate to the U.S. for a better life. Like hundreds of thousands of others, she is caught in limbo, trapped in red tape by a country that offers promise but too often overlooks the potential of those who play by the rules. Only a few hundred thousand work visa's are approved each fiscal year, compared to the millions crossing the U.S. border illegally every year. (1911. 8 U.S.C. 1325)

Throughout her journey, Ethel faces intense moments of doubt and despair, but she never loses sight of the hope that has driven her since her childhood and the prospect of a better life is possible. Through her story readers are reminded of the resilience of the human spirit, the sacrifices people make in the pursuit of a better future, and the immense challenges that immigrants, especially educated, skilled professionals can face when they try to navigate a complex and often unfair system

In the end, Ethel's Journey is not just about one woman's fight for a better life; it is a powerful commentary on the experiences of millions of people struggling for a place in the land of opportunity, people who, despite the odds, continue to dream.

Photographs 2013 by Ethel Ocaña

Ethel's typhoon damaged nursing college books air drying. College classes will resume eventually.

Nov 2013

In 2012 Ethel, already a Registered Midwife, had ambitions to further her education. She decided to go back to college to become a Registered Nurse.

But not long after, in November 2013, Typhoon Haiyan hit the island of Leyte directly over Ethel's home. This Category 5 typhoon killed over 10,000 people from nearby islands washing thousands of dead bodies up on the shoreline of Tacloban City. Typhoon Haiyan was the most powerful of 11 typhoons that hit Philippines in 2013 with winds up to 190/mph or 305/kph. In comparison to Hurricane Milton, in October 2024, had winds of 180/mph or 289/kph.

During the days that followed, Ethel and her family and indeed the entire island had no electricity. Ethel remembers standing in front 578 Mall watching Anderson Coopers CNN news report several days after. Everyone was so proud and grateful to see Anderson Cooper, as he appeared to be the only one at the time reporting on the devastation and showing the world the suffering that everyone was enduring. To this day the victims still believe Anderson Coopers coverage was responsible for sparking the massive humanitarian mission that eventually involved military aid from around the world.

The smell of the thousands of decomposing bodies was overwhelming the entire city of Tacloban and was actually becoming a health hazard for the community. Over the next weeks the Philippine government deployed 10 wheeler dump trucks to carry away all the dead bodies.

Due to the extensive calamity caused by the typhoon, Ethel's college program was delayed.

Photographs 2013 by Ethel Ocaña

Ethel's Dad repairing roof one day after Typhoon Haiyan 2013 before evacuation to Cebu City

Photographs 2019 by Ethel Ocaña

Ethels Mom 75 Dad 73

After several days with no outside help, people became desperate for water and food. Fortunately, within a few days Joint Task Force Operation Damayan (JTF 505) began bringing in food and water and started evacuating the locals from Tacloban City to the nearby island city of Cebu and Manila. Over 2,000 tons of relief supplies were brought in and over 21,000 people were evacuated in less than a month.

Ethel and her family were finally evacuated about two weeks after Haiyan while her mother and father remained in Tacloban.

Imagine if you have ever been in South Florida in the middle of summer, with no electricity or fans during the hottest part of summer. This is the normal temperature in the Philippines all year round. Temps of over 95 F (35 C), day and night, for 12 months with no fans, no AC, and endless clouds of biting insects plagued the residents of the area.

Electricity was not restored to Tacloban City for nearly 12 months after Haiyan hit.

The United States played a key role in providing immediate relief and support, not just in physical supplies, but in the emotional healing that came from seeing American personnel and civilians working alongside Filipinos in the wake of such a disaster.

Ethels neighborhood

Photographs 2013 by Ethel Ocaña

After spending a few weeks in Cebu City Ethel's father had a stroke so, the family returned home to Tacloban City despite its lack of services.

Their home was damaged but livable. The family remained on the ground floor of the damaged house. Ethel's father remained in the hospital recovering from his stroke.

Ethel and her brothers began making whatever repairs they could to make the damaged house more comfortable.

With no electricity and barely drinkable water, the only life that thrived on the island then was the millions of mosquitoes biting day and night, as well as all the turkeys and chickens that survived the typhoon. The mosquitoes endured; the poultry, however, did not long survive return of the starving families.

In 2013/2014, while waiting for college to resume, Ethel secured a job with a French humanitarian organization assisting with psychosocial intervention therapy with the mental health and trauma caused by Typhoon Haiyan. After a while, she then transitioned to a different French humanitarian organization coordinating the rebuilding of the infrastructure for water throughout the city of Tacloban. Ethel quickly rose to become the regional manager, acting as a liaison between the French humanitarian organization and her local barangay leaders and captains.

Although a bitter sweet occupation, Ethel enjoyed helping her community while at the same time Ethel was coping with the exact same trauma for which she was providing therapy to others.

"The soul becomes dyed with the color of its thoughts."
- Marcus Aurelius, Meditations

Ethel standing at Gen MacArthur Monument
Palo Leyte Philippines Nov 2024

In September 2020 Ethel's mother was rushed to a neighboring hospital. Due to the ongoing lockdown and quarantine restrictions from the COVID-19 pandemic then underway, Ethel was not allowed to leave her clinical rotation. If she did, she faced being dropped from the nursing program. She could not imagine the pain her mother was enduring, alone in a hospital bed, without her daughter or any family to offer comfort or support. Yet, as she sat in the hospital for her clinicals, with her own heart breaking, she recognized that if she left the hospital to be with her mother, she would lose everything she had worked so hard for. Unfortunately, despite the doctors' efforts, Ethel's mom passed away less than 24 hours after arriving the hospital.

Just a few months later, in December, Ethel graduated RN school with a bachelor's degree. Ethel immediately began working as an Operating Room Perioperative Nurse in the tiny Philippine province of Tacloban City, on the island of Leyte, where her family lived.

This was the same island where General MacArthur had waded ashore on October 20, 1944 to fulfil his promise to the people of Philippines that he would return and restore the local government back to the Philippine people after the Japanese occupation.

The resilience and generosity of the American people during the return of General MacArthur and Typhoon Haiyan's aftermath left a deep impression on Ethel.

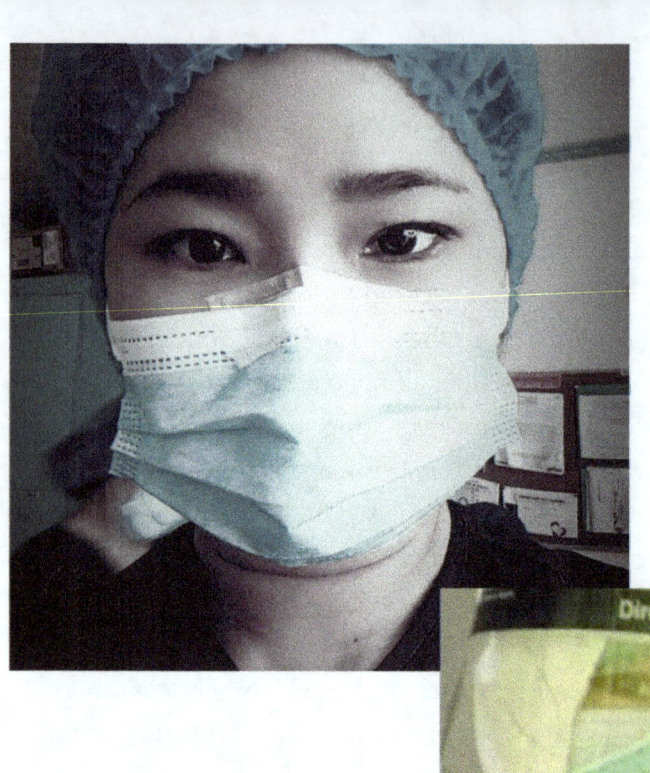

Ethel on duty as a nursing student
during Covid
2020

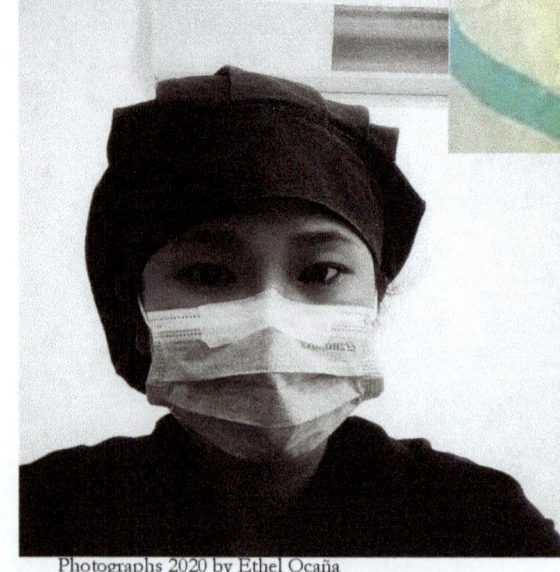

Photographs 2020 by Ethel Ocaña

Ethel applied to take the US nursing exam known as NCLEX. She had a tough time with the exam but passed the NCLEX in December 2022. This was a vital step towards demonstrating her qualifications to emigrate to the U.S.

Ethel's strong desire to provide humanitarian support for others allowed her the opportunity to volunteer for medical missions in the most poverty-stricken rural provinces throughout the Philippine archipelago. There is no shortage of these, as the Philippines is comprised of over 7,000 islands, many of which have no access to medical facilities.

All of the medical missions are voluntary and require long 15 to 20 hour days over a 2 or 3 day mission. The teams of doctors and nurses come from hospitals all over the Philippines. Teams provide free surgical procedures to people who otherwise would never even see a hospital. From AV Fistula creation to cyst removals to OB/GYN procedures, including hysterectomies and many other minor surgical procedures, these teams work tirelessly to care for up to a thousand patients in a 3 day span.

Photograph 2023 by Ethel Ocaña

Ethel Modeling

"To be like the rock that the waves keep crashing over. It stands unmoved and the raging of the sea falls still around it."

- Marcus Aurelius, Meditations

In January 2023 Ethel filed a EB-3 immigration visa application to work as a registered nurse in New York State.

Everything was completed for the U.S. work visa, and Ethel was assigned a Priority Date (PD) of March 2023. However, this date is somewhat misleading. She has been following the U.S. Visa Bulletin for the entire FY23, FY24 and FY25. Ever since April 2024 the PD has not advanced past November 2022.

PD must reach March 2023 for Ethel to be allowed an interview with the immigration officers in Manila Philippines, a required part of her application.

In early 2024 Ethel endured the other aspects of the rigorous U.S. visa process.

Background investigations and medical checkup, which took a full day, including a physical exam consisting of carrying a 40lb weight around for 30 minutes while doing various physical activities. For reference Ethel is 5'2" 105 pounds. She was even required to strip down naked on two separate occasions to be check in every crevasse of her body and probed by the physician conducting the exam.

In addition, Ethel was required to have a Tuberculosis (TB) test and X-ray to determine that she never had TB.

Once Ethel's PD is reached she will be required to undergo a third complete medical physical before final approval. Ethel's education has already been verified by the New York Board of Nursing.

These are all U.S. immigration work visa requirements.

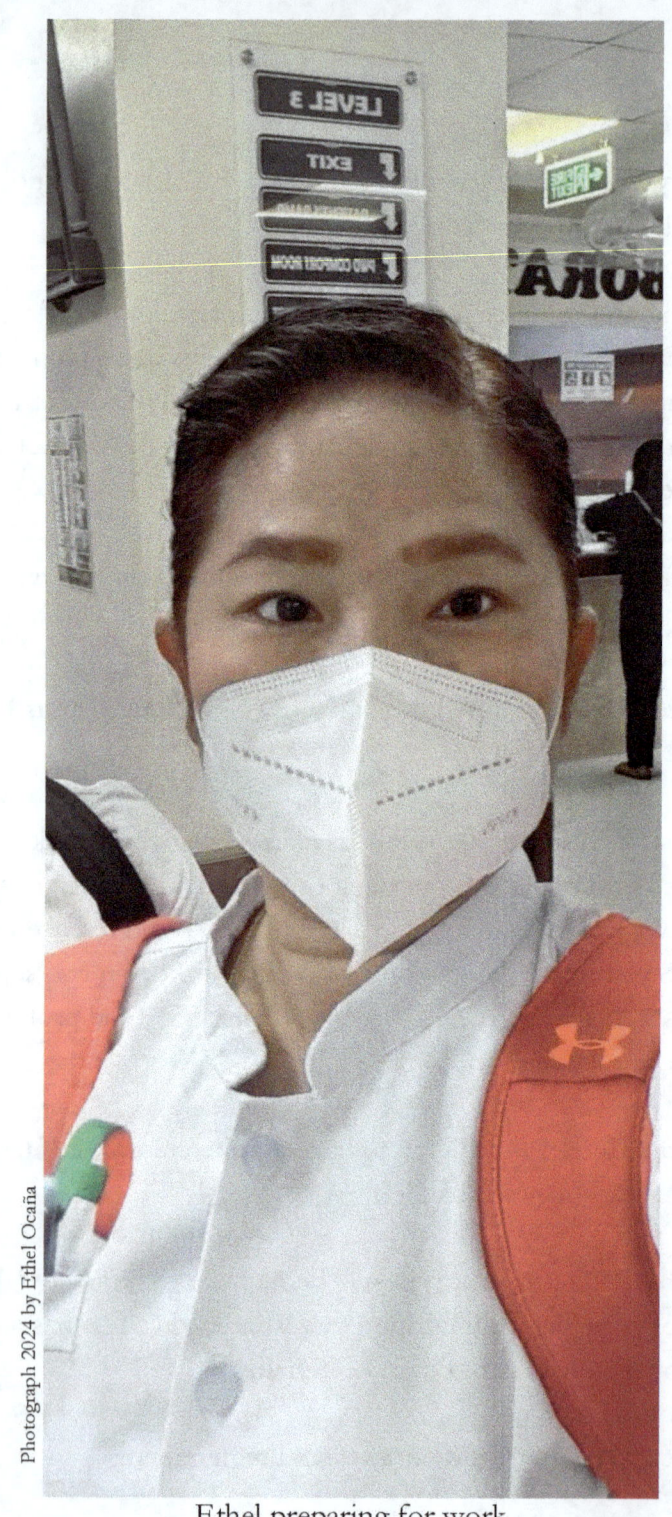

Photograph 2024 by Ethel Ocaña

Ethel preparing for work
July 2024

Currently as of February 2025 Ethel is still working in the Philippines as a Perioperative RN working in Surgery as a Pre-op Nurse, OR Circulator Nurse, PACU Nurse and Scrub Nurse.

The updated list of PD for February 2025 still remains at November 2022.

The total costs are currently around $4,000 USD and are expected to increase before final approval. These expenses include multiple round trip flights to Manila for mandatory immigration medical and physical exams, as well as additional trips to Cebu for mandatory training on three separate occasions. On top of that, there is the added burden of lost work hours to attend these required trainings, all without any reimbursement.

Meanwhile, the world watches as millions of unvetted immigrants "illegally" cross the southern border of the United States. These individuals undergo no background investigations, no criminal history checks, no medical examinations, and bring with them unknown levels of education and medical histories.

Photograph 2023 Philippines Flag by Ethel Ocaña

Photograph 2023 by Josh Bannister

How is the United States of America so strict with LEGAL work visa immigrants requiring background investigation, extensive and invasive medical requirements and education requirements, but so carefree when it comes to millions of immigrants crossing the U.S. southern border "illegally"? (1911. 8 U.S.C. 1325)

Ethel and tens of thousands of other professionals are struggling to complete the U.S. work visa process the legal way and yet they are being left behind.

Something needs to change.

Nemo Resideo

Ethel after a 14 hour shift.
190 Philippine Peso (Php) per hour.
Equivelant to $3 USD per hour.

Immigration Statistics

2023 - Over 11 million immigrants are in the U.S. illegally. Of those over 600,000 are females under the age of 18

Office of Homeland Security Statistics
U.S. Department Office of Homeland Security
ohss.dhs.gov, April 2024

Mass, uncontrolled immigration is especially unfair to the many wonderful, law-abiding immigrants already living here who followed the rules and waited their turn. Some have been waiting for many years. Some have been waiting for a long time. They've done everything perfectly. And they're going to come in. At some point, they're going to come in. In many cases, very soon. We need them to come in, because we have companies coming into our country; they need workers. But they have to come in on a merit basis, and they will come in on a merit basis.

- President Donald J. Trump, November 1, 2018, Remarks by President Trump on the Illegal Immigration Crisis and Border Security, Roosevelt Room
   https://trumpwhitehouse.archives.gov/briefings-statements/remarks-president-trump-illegal-immigration-crisis-border-security/

The following pages are screenshots showing the progression and retrogression of the Priority Date (PD) from Oct 2022 to Dec 2024, for reference only.

<u>Travel.State.Gov</u>
U.S. DEPARTMENT of STATE — BUREAU of CONSULAR AFFAIRS
Website as of November 2024

All Americans, not only in the states most heavily affected, but in every place in the country are rightly disturbed by the large numbers of illegal aliens entering our country. The jobs they hold might otherwise be held by citizens or legal immigrants. The public services they use impose burdens on our taxpayers. That's why our administration has moved aggressively to secure our borders more by hiring a record number of new border guards. By deporting twice as many criminal aliens as ever before. By cracking down on illegal hiring. By barring welfare benefits to illegal aliens. In the budget I will present to you we will try to do more to speed the deportation of illegal aliens who are arrested for crimes. To better identify illegal aliens in the work place as recommended by the commission headed by former Congresswoman Barbara Jordan. We are a nation of immigrants but we are also a nation of laws. It is wrong and ultimately self defeating for a nation of immigrants to permit the kind of abuse of our immigration laws we have seen in recent years and we must do more to stop it.

- President Bill Clinton, 1995, SOTU C-SPAN
  https://www.c-span.org/clip/joint-session-of-congress/user-clip-clinton-1995-immigration-sotu/4351026

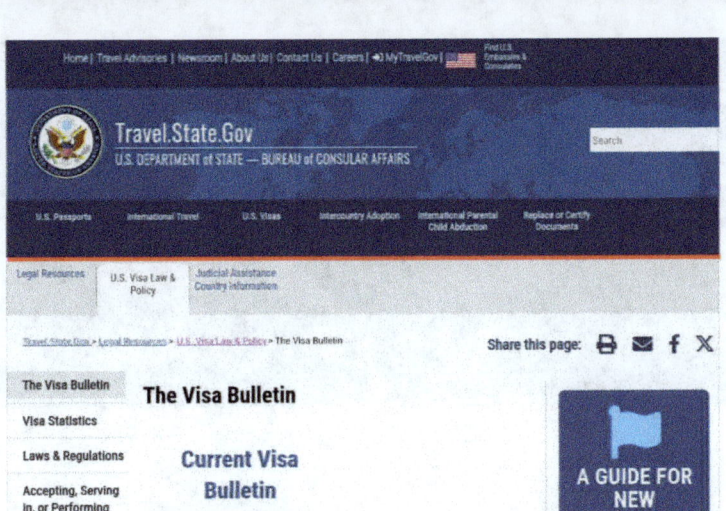

The Visa Bulletin

Current Visa Bulletin

 November 2024

Upcoming Visa Bulletin

 December 2024

NOTE: The Final Action Dates and Dates for Filing published within the *Visa Bulletins* on this site are listed in the DAY-MONTH-YEAR *(dd-mmm-yy)* format.

USCIS, in coordination with Department of State (State), is revising the procedures for determining visa availability for applicants waiting to file for employment-based or family-sponsored preference adjustment of status. The revised process will better align with procedures State uses for foreign nationals who seek to become U.S. permanent residents by applying for immigrant visas at U.S. consulates and embassies abroad.

See more information on the changes here: **USCIS Announces Revised Procedures for Determining Visa Availability for Applicants Waiting to File for Adjustment of Status.**

Archived *Visa Bulletins*: Online versions of the *Visa Bulletin* are for informational purposes only and

Screenshots for reference only.

Copyright Information

Links to travel.state.gov are welcomed. Unless a copyright is indicated, information on the Consular Affairs web site is in the public domain and may be copied and distributed without permission. Citation of the Bureau of Consular Affairs, U.S. State Department as source of the information is appreciated.

If a copyright is indicated on a photo, graphic, or other material, permission to copy these materials must be obtained from the original source. For photos without captions or with only partial captions, hold your cursor over the photo to view the "alt tag" for any copyright information. Please note that many photos used on this website are copyrighted. Please note that the U.S. Government has an international copyright on Country Commercial Guides.

A. FINAL ACTION DATES FOR EMPLOYMENT-BASED PREFERENCE CASES

On the chart below, the listing of a date for any class indicates that the class is oversubscribed (see paragraph 1); "C" means current, i.e., numbers are authorized for issuance to all qualified applicants; and "U" means unauthorized, i.e., numbers are not authorized for issuance. (NOTE: Numbers are authorized for issuance only for applicants whose priority date is **earlier** than the final action date listed below.)

Oct 2022 FY23

Employment-based	All Chargeability Areas Except Those Listed	CHINA-mainland born	EL SALVADOR GUATEMALA HONDURAS	INDIA	MEXICO	PHILIPPINES
1st	C	C	C	C	C	C
2nd	C	08JUN19	C	01APR12	C	C
3rd	C	15JUN18	C	01APR12	C	C
Other Workers	01JUN20	01SEP12	01JUN20	01APR12	01JUN20	01JUN20
4th	C	C	15MAR18	C	15SEP20	C
Certain Religious Workers	U	U	U	U	U	U
5th Unreserved (including C5, T5, I5, R5)	C	22MAR15	C	08NOV19	C	C
5th Set Aside: Rural (20%)	C	C	C	C	C	C
5th Set Aside: High Unemployment (10%)	C	C	C	C	C	C
5th Set Aside: Infrastructure (2%)	C	C	C	C	C	C

*Employment Third Preference Other Workers Category: Section 203(e) of the Nicaraguan and Central American Relief Act (NACARA) passed by Congress in November 1997, as amended by Section 1(e) of Pub. L. 105-139, provides that once the Employment Third Preference Other Worker (EW) cut-off date has reached the priority date of the latest EW petition approved prior to November 19, 1997, the 10,000 EW numbers available for a fiscal year are to be reduced by up to 5,000 annually beginning in the following fiscal year. This reduction is to be made for as long as necessary to offset adjustments under the NACARA program. Since the EW final action date reached November 19, 1997 during Fiscal Year 2001, the reduction in the EW annual limit to 5,000 began in Fiscal Year 2002. For Fiscal Year 2022 this reduction will be limited to approximately 150.

First you've got to toughen border security. You can't continue to have open borders. And you've got to promote personnel and technology along the borders to make sure we know who's coming in to our country and prevent people from entering illegally. I think everybody should agree with that. That to me has got to be priority one. Priority two you've got to crack down on employers who employ undocumented workers. People wouldn't come here if there weren't jobs waiting for them.

 - Hillary Clinton, Town Hall in Iowa November 7, 2007
    https://www.nytimes.com/video/us/politics/1194817098972/hillary-clinton-on-immigration.html

A. FINAL ACTION DATES FOR EMPLOYMENT-BASED PREFERENCE CASES

On the chart below, the listing of a date for any class indicates that the class is oversubscribed (see paragraph 1); "C" means current, i.e., numbers are authorized for issuance to all qualified applicants; and "U" means unauthorized, i.e., numbers are not authorized for issuance. (NOTE: Numbers are authorized for issuance only for applicants whose priority date is **earlier** than the final action date listed below.)

Nov 2022 FY23

Employment-based	All Chargeability Areas Except Those Listed	CHINA-mainland born	EL SALVADOR GUATEMALA HONDURAS	INDIA	MEXICO	PHILIPPINES
1st	C	C	C	C	C	C
2nd	C	08JUN19	C	01APR12	C	C
3rd	C	15JUN18	C	01APR12	C	C
Other Workers	01JUN20	01DEC12	01JUN20	01APR12	01JUN20	01JUN20
4th	C	C	15MAR18	C	15SEP20	C
Certain Religious Workers	C	C	15MAR18	C	15SEP20	C
5th Unreserved (including C5, T5, I5, R5)	C	22MAR15	C	08NOV19	C	C
5th Set Aside: Rural (20%)	C	C	C	C	C	C
5th Set Aside: High Unemployment (10%)	C	C	C	C	C	C
5th Set Aside: Infrastructure (2%)	C	C	C	C	C	C

*Employment Third Preference Other Workers Category: Section 203(e) of the Nicaraguan and Central American Relief Act (NACARA) passed by Congress in November 1997, as amended by Section 1(e) of Pub. L. 105-139, provides that once the Employment Third Preference Other Worker (EW) cut-off date has reached the priority date of the latest EW petition approved prior to November 19, 1997, the 10,000 EW numbers available for a fiscal year are to be reduced by up to 5,000 annually beginning in the following fiscal year. This reduction is to be made for as long as necessary to offset adjustments under the NACARA program. Since the EW final action date reached November 19, 1997 during Fiscal Year 2001, the reduction in the EW annual limit to 5,000 began in Fiscal Year 2002. For Fiscal Year 2022 this reduction will be limited to approximately 150.

Today our immigration system is broken. And everybody knows it. Families who enter our country the right way and play by the rules watch others flout the rules. Business owners who offer their workers good wages and benefits see the competition exploit undocumented immigrants by paying them far less. All of us take offense to anyone who reaps the rewards of living in America without taking on the responsibilities of living in America.

 - President Barrack Obama, November 20, 2014, The Obama Whitehouse Youtube Channel.
https://www.youtube.com/watch?v=6Q_Xk66gsRU

A. FINAL ACTION DATES FOR EMPLOYMENT-BASED PREFERENCE CASES

On the chart below, the listing of a date for any class indicates that the class is oversubscribed (see paragraph 1); "C" means current, i.e., numbers are authorized for issuance to all qualified applicants; and "U" means unauthorized, i.e., numbers are not authorized for issuance. (NOTE: Numbers are authorized for issuance only for applicants whose priority date is **earlier** than the final action date listed below.)

Dec 2022 FY23

Employment-based	All Chargeability Areas Except Those Listed	CHINA-mainland born	EL SALVADOR GUATEMALA HONDURAS	INDIA	MEXICO	PHILIPPINES
1st	C	C	C	C	C	C
2nd	01NOV22	08JUN19	01NOV22	08OCT11	01NOV22	01NOV22
3rd	C	01AUG18	C	15JUN12	C	C
Other Workers	01JUN20	22JUN13	01JUN20	15JUN12	01JUN20	01JUN20
4th	22JUN22	22JUN22	15MAR18	22JUN22	15SEP20	22JUN22
Certain Religious Workers	22JUN22	22JUN22	15MAR18	22JUN22	15SEP20	22JUN22
5th Unreserved (including C5, T5, I5, R5)	C	22MAR15	C	08NOV19	C	C
5th Set Aside: Rural (20%)	C	C	C	C	C	C
5th Set Aside: High Unemployment (10%)	C	C	C	C	C	C
5th Set Aside: Infrastructure (2%)	C	C	C	C	C	C

*Employment Third Preference Other Workers Category: Section 203(e) of the Nicaraguan and Central American Relief Act (NACARA) passed by Congress in November 1997, as amended by Section 1(e) of Pub. L. 105-139, provides that once the Employment Third Preference Other Worker (EW) cut-off date has reached the priority date of the latest EW petition approved prior to November 19, 1997, the 10,000 EW numbers available for a fiscal year are to be reduced by up to 5,000 annually beginning in the following fiscal year. This reduction is to be made for as long as necessary to offset adjustments under the NACARA program. Since the EW final action date reached November 19, 1997 during Fiscal Year 2001, the reduction in the EW annual limit to 5,000 began in Fiscal Year 2002. For Fiscal Year 2022 this reduction will be limited to approximately 150.

The Immigration Act of 1990

Recommends a tripartite immigration policy that permits the entry of nuclear family members, professional and skilled workers.... The commission emphasizes nuclear family......

I urge the congress to adopt tough policies needed to verify employment authorization. What the commission is concerned about are the unskilled workers in our society in an age in which unskilled workers have far too few opportunities open to them. When immigrants are less well educated and less skilled they may pose economic hardships for the most vulnerable of Americans particularly those who are unemployed or underemployed and the commission sees no justification to the continued entry of unskilled foreign workers......

- Barbara Jordan Texas, (D) Youtube C-SPAN2 1995
  https://youtu.be/TMywOal05s0?si=xMQ9J9hMMiAcynpy

A. FINAL ACTION DATES FOR EMPLOYMENT-BASED PREFERENCE CASES

On the chart below, the listing of a date for any class indicates that the class is oversubscribed (see paragraph 1); "C" means current, i.e., numbers are authorized for issuance to all qualified applicants; and "U" means unauthorized, i.e., numbers are not authorized for issuance. (NOTE: Numbers are authorized for issuance only for applicants whose priority date is **earlier** than the final action date listed below.)

Employment-based	All Chargeability Areas Except Those Listed	CHINA-mainland born	EL SALVADOR GUATEMALA HONDURAS	INDIA	MEXICO	PHILIPPINES
1st	C	01FEB22	C	01FEB22	C	C
2nd	01NOV22	08JUN19	01NOV22	08OCT11	01NOV22	01NOV22
3rd	C	01AUG18	C	15JUN12	C	C
Other Workers	01JUN20	22DEC13	01JUN20	15JUN12	01JUN20	01JUN20
4th	22JUN22	22JUN22	15MAR18	22JUN22	15SEP20	22JUN22
Certain Religious Workers	U	U	U	U	U	U
5th Unreserved (including C5, T5, I5, R5)	C	22MAR15	C	08NOV19	C	C
5th Set Aside: Rural (20%)	C	C	C	C	C	C
5th Set Aside: High Unemployment (10%)	C	C	C	C	C	C
5th Set Aside: Infrastructure (2%)	C	C	C	C	C	C

*Employment Third Preference Other Workers Category: Section 203(e) of the Nicaraguan and Central American Relief Act (NACARA) passed by Congress in November 1997, as amended by Section 1(e) of Pub. L. 105-139, provides that once the Employment Third Preference Other Worker (EW) cut-off date has reached the priority date of the latest EW petition approved prior to November 19, 1997, the 10,000 EW numbers available for a fiscal year are to be reduced by up to 5,000 annually beginning in the following fiscal year. This reduction is to be made for as long as necessary to offset adjustments under the NACARA program. Since the EW final action date reached November 19, 1997 during Fiscal Year 2001, the reduction in the EW annual limit to 5,000 began in Fiscal Year 2002. For Fiscal Year 2022 this reduction will be limited to approximately 150.

A. FINAL ACTION DATES FOR EMPLOYMENT-BASED PREFERENCE CASES

On the chart below, the listing of a date for any class indicates that the class is oversubscribed (see paragraph 1); "C" means current, i.e., numbers are authorized for issuance to all qualified applicants; and "U" means unauthorized, i.e., numbers are not authorized for issuance. (NOTE: Numbers are authorized for issuance only for applicants whose priority date is **earlier** than the final action date listed below.)

Feb 2023 FY23

Employment-based	All Chargeability Areas Except Those Listed	CHINA-mainland born	EL SALVADOR GUATEMALA HONDURAS	INDIA	MEXICO	PHILIPPINES
1st	C	01FEB22	C	01FEB22	C	C
2nd	01NOV22	08JUN19	01NOV22	08OCT11	01NOV22	01NOV22
3rd	C	01AUG18	C	15JUN12	C	C
Other Workers	01JAN20	22DEC13	01JAN20	15JUN12	01JAN20	01JAN20
4th	22JUN22	22JUN22	15MAR18	22JUN22	15SEP20	22JUN22
Certain Religious Workers	22JUN22	22JUN22	15MAR18	22JUN22	15SEP20	22JUN22
5th Unreserved (including C5, T5, I5, R5)	C	22MAR15	C	08NOV19	C	C
5th Set Aside: Rural (20%)	C	C	C	C	C	C
5th Set Aside: High Unemployment (10%)	C	C	C	C	C	C
5th Set Aside: Infrastructure (2%)	C	C	C	C	C	C

*Employment Third Preference Other Workers Category: Section 203(e) of the Nicaraguan and Central American Relief Act (NACARA) passed by Congress in November 1997, as amended by Section 1(e) of Pub. L. 105-139, provides that once the Employment Third Preference Other Worker (EW) cut-off date has reached the priority date of the latest EW petition approved prior to November 19, 1997, the 10,000 EW numbers available for a fiscal year are to be reduced by up to 5,000 annually beginning in the following fiscal year. This reduction is to be made for as long as necessary to offset adjustments under the NACARA program. Since the EW final action date reached November 19, 1997 during Fiscal Year 2001, the reduction in the EW annual limit to 5,000 began in Fiscal Year 2002. For Fiscal Year 2023 this reduction will be limited to approximately 150.

A. FINAL ACTION DATES FOR EMPLOYMENT-BASED PREFERENCE CASES

On the chart below, the listing of a date for any class indicates that the class is oversubscribed (see paragraph 1); "C" means current, i.e., numbers are authorized for issuance to all qualified applicants; and "U" means unauthorized, i.e., numbers are not authorized for issuance. (NOTE: Numbers are authorized for issuance only for applicants whose priority date is **earlier** than the final action date listed below.)

Mar 2023 FY23

Employment-based	All Chargeability Areas Except Those Listed	CHINA-mainland born	EL SALVADOR GUATEMALA HONDURAS	INDIA	MEXICO	PHILIPPINES
1st	C	01FEB22	C	01FEB22	C	C
2nd	01NOV22	08JUN19	01NOV22	08OCT11	01NOV22	01NOV22
3rd	C	01AUG18	C	15JUN12	C	C
Other Workers	01JAN20	01JUL14	01JAN20	15JUN12	01JAN20	01JAN20
4th	01FEB22	01FEB22	15MAR18	01MAR21	01AUG20	01FEB22
Certain Religious Workers	01FEB22	01FEB22	15MAR18	01MAR21	01AUG20	01FEB22
5th Unreserved (including C5, T5, I5, R5)	C	08JUL15	C	01JUN18	C	C
5th Set Aside: Rural (20%)	C	C	C	C	C	C
5th Set Aside: High Unemployment (10%)	C	C	C	C	C	C
5th Set Aside: Infrastructure (2%)	C	C	C	C	C	C

*Employment Third Preference Other Workers Category: Section 203(e) of the Nicaraguan and Central American Relief Act (NACARA) passed by Congress in November 1997, as amended by Section 1(e) of Pub. L. 105-139, provides that once the Employment Third Preference Other Worker (EW) cut-off date has reached the priority date of the latest EW petition approved prior to November 19, 1997, the 10,000 EW numbers available for a fiscal year are to be reduced by up to 5,000 annually beginning in the following fiscal year. This reduction is to be made for as long as necessary to offset adjustments under the NACARA program. Since the EW final action date reached November 19, 1997 during Fiscal Year 2001, the reduction in the EW annual limit to 5,000 began in Fiscal Year 2002. For Fiscal Year 2023 this reduction will be limited to approximately 150.

A. FINAL ACTION DATES FOR EMPLOYMENT-BASED PREFERENCE CASES

On the chart below, the listing of a date for any class indicates that the class is oversubscribed (see paragraph 1); "C" means current, i.e., numbers are authorized for issuance to all qualified applicants; and "U" means unauthorized, i.e., numbers are not authorized for issuance. (NOTE: Numbers are authorized for issuance only for applicants whose priority date is **earlier** than the final action date listed below.)

Employment-based	All Chargeability Areas Except Those Listed	CHINA-mainland born	INDIA	MEXICO	PHILIPPINES
1st	C	01FEB22	01FEB22	C	C
2nd	01JUL22	08JUN19	01JAN11	01JUL22	01JUL22
3rd	C	01NOV18	15JUN12	C	C
Other Workers	01JAN20	01OCT14	15JUN12	01JAN20	01JAN20
4th	01SEP18	01SEP18	01SEP18	01SEP18	01SEP18
Certain Religious Workers	01SEP18	01SEP18	01SEP18	01SEP18	01SEP18
5th Unreserved (including C5, T5, I5, R5)	C	08JUL15	01JUN18	C	C
5th Set Aside: Rural (20%)	C	C	C	C	C
5th Set Aside: High Unemployment (10%)	C	C	C	C	C
5th Set Aside: Infrastructure (2%)	C	C	C	C	C

*Employment Third Preference Other Workers Category: Section 203(e) of the Nicaraguan and Central American Relief Act (NACARA) passed by Congress in November 1997, as amended by Section 1(e) of Pub. L. 105-139, provides that once the Employment Third Preference Other Worker (EW) cut-off date has reached the priority date of the latest EW petition approved prior to November 19, 1997, the 10,000 EW numbers available for a fiscal year are to be reduced by up to 5,000 annually beginning in the following fiscal year. This reduction is to be made for as long as necessary to offset adjustments under the NACARA program. Since the EW final action date reached November 19, 1997 during Fiscal Year 2001, the reduction in the EW annual limit to 5,000 began in Fiscal Year 2002. For Fiscal Year 2023 this reduction will be limited to approximately 150.

A. FINAL ACTION DATES FOR EMPLOYMENT-BASED PREFERENCE CASES

On the chart below, the listing of a date for any class indicates that the class is oversubscribed (see paragraph 1); "C" means current, i.e., numbers are authorized for issuance to all qualified applicants; and "U" means unauthorized, i.e., numbers are not authorized for issuance. (NOTE: Numbers are authorized for issuance only for applicants whose priority date is **earlier** than the final action date listed below.)

May 2023 FY23

Employment-based	All Chargeability Areas Except Those Listed	CHINA-mainland born	INDIA	MEXICO	PHILIPPINES
1st	C	01FEB22	01FEB22	C	C
2nd	15FEB22	08JUN19	01JAN11	15FEB22	15FEB22
3rd	01JUN22	01APR19	15JUN12	01JUN22	01JUN22
Other Workers	01JAN20	15APR15	15JUN12	01JAN20	01JAN20
4th	01SEP18	01SEP18	01SEP18	01SEP18	01SEP18
Certain Religious Workers	01SEP18	01SEP18	01SEP18	01SEP18	01SEP18
5th Unreserved (including C5, T5, I5, R5)	C	08SEP15	01JUN18	C	C
5th Set Aside: Rural (20%)	C	C	C	C	C
5th Set Aside: High Unemployment (10%)	C	C	C	C	C
5th Set Aside: Infrastructure (2%)	C	C	C	C	C

*Employment Third Preference Other Workers Category: Section 203(e) of the Nicaraguan and Central American Relief Act (NACARA) passed by Congress in November 1997, as amended by Section 1(e) of Pub. L. 105-139, provides that once the Employment Third Preference Other Worker (EW) cut-off date has reached the priority date of the latest EW petition approved prior to November 19, 1997, the 10,000 EW numbers available for a fiscal year are to be reduced by up to 5,000 annually beginning in the following fiscal year. This reduction is to be made for as long as necessary to offset adjustments under the NACARA program. Since the EW final action date reached November 19, 1997 during Fiscal Year 2001, the reduction in the EW annual limit to 5,000 began in Fiscal Year 2002. For Fiscal Year 2023 this reduction will be limited to approximately 150.

A. **FINAL ACTION DATES FOR EMPLOYMENT-BASED PREFERENCE CASES**

On the chart below, the listing of a date for any class indicates that the class is oversubscribed (see paragraph 1); "C" means current, i.e., numbers are authorized for issuance to all qualified applicants; and "U" means unauthorized, i.e., numbers are not authorized for issuance. (NOTE: Numbers are authorized for issuance only for applicants whose priority date is **earlier** than the final action date listed below.)

Employment-based	All Chargeability Areas Except Those Listed	CHINA-mainland born	INDIA	MEXICO	PHILIPPINES
1st	C	01FEB22	01FEB22	C	C
2nd	15FEB22	08JUN19	01JAN11	15FEB22	15FEB22
3rd	01JUN22	01APR19	15JUN12	01JUN22	01JUN22
Other Workers	01JAN20	01SEP15	15JUN12	01JAN20	01JAN20
4th	01SEP18	01SEP18	01SEP18	01SEP18	01SEP18
Certain Religious Workers	01SEP18	01SEP18	01SEP18	01SEP18	01SEP18
5th Unreserved (including C5, T5, I5, R5)	C	08SEP15	01APR17	C	C
5th Set Aside: Rural (20%)	C	C	C	C	C
5th Set Aside: High Unemployment (10%)	C	C	C	C	C
5th Set Aside: Infrastructure (2%)	C	C	C	C	C

*Employment Third Preference Other Workers Category: Section 203(e) of the Nicaraguan and Central American Relief Act (NACARA) passed by Congress in November 1997, as amended by Section 1(e) of Pub. L. 105-139, provides that once the Employment Third Preference Other Worker (EW) cut-off date has reached the priority date of the latest EW petition approved prior to November 19, 1997, the 10,000 EW numbers available for a fiscal year are to be reduced by up to 5,000 annually beginning in the following fiscal year. This reduction is to be made for as long as necessary to offset adjustments under the NACARA program. Since the EW final action date reached November 19, 1997 during Fiscal Year 2001, the reduction in the EW annual limit to 5,000 began in Fiscal Year 2002. For Fiscal Year 2023 this reduction will be limited to approximately 150.

A. **FINAL ACTION DATES FOR EMPLOYMENT-BASED PREFERENCE CASES**

On the chart below, the listing of a date for any class indicates that the class is oversubscribed (see paragraph 1); "C" means current, i.e., numbers are authorized for issuance to all qualified applicants; and "U" means unauthorized, i.e., numbers are not authorized for issuance. (NOTE: Numbers are authorized for issuance only for applicants whose priority date is **earlier** than the final action date listed below.)

Employment-based	All Chargeability Areas Except Those Listed	CHINA-mainland born	INDIA	MEXICO	PHILIPPINES
1st	C	01FEB22	01FEB22	C	C
2nd	15FEB22	08JUN19	01JAN11	15FEB22	15FEB22
3rd	01FEB22	01APR19	01JAN09	01FEB22	01FEB22
Other Workers	01JAN20	01SEP15	01JAN09	01JAN20	01JAN20
4th	01SEP18	01SEP18	01SEP18	01SEP18	01SEP18
Certain Religious Workers	01SEP18	01SEP18	01SEP18	01SEP18	01SEP18
5th Unreserved (including C5, T5, I5, R5)	C	08SEP15	01APR17	C	C
5th Set Aside: Rural (20%)	C	C	C	C	C
5th Set Aside: High Unemployment (10%)	C	C	C	C	C
5th Set Aside: Infrastructure (2%)	C	C	C	C	C

*Employment Third Preference Other Workers Category: Section 203(e) of the Nicaraguan and Central American Relief Act (NACARA) passed by Congress in November 1997, as amended by Section 1(e) of Pub. L. 105-139, provides that once the Employment Third Preference Other Worker (EW) cut-off date has reached the priority date of the latest EW petition approved prior to November 19, 1997, the 10,000 EW numbers available for a fiscal year are to be reduced by up to 5,000 annually beginning in the following fiscal year. This reduction is to be made for as long as necessary to offset adjustments under the NACARA program. Since the EW final action date reached November 19, 1997 during Fiscal Year 2001, the reduction in the EW annual limit to 5,000 began in Fiscal Year 2002. For Fiscal Year 2023 this reduction will be limited to approximately 150.

A. FINAL ACTION DATES FOR EMPLOYMENT-BASED PREFERENCE CASES

On the chart below, the listing of a date for any class indicates that the class is oversubscribed (see paragraph 1); "C" means current, i.e., numbers are authorized for issuance to all qualified applicants; and "U" means unauthorized, i.e., numbers are not authorized for issuance. (NOTE: Numbers are authorized for issuance only for applicants whose priority date is **earlier** than the final action date listed below.)

Aug 2023 FY23

Employment-based	All Chargeability Areas Except Those Listed	CHINA-mainland born	INDIA	MEXICO	PHILIPPINES
1st	01AUG23	01FEB22	01JAN12	01AUG23	01AUG23
2nd	01APR22	08JUL19	01JAN11	01APR22	01APR22
3rd	01MAY20	01JUN19	01JAN09	01MAY20	01MAY20
Other Workers	01MAY20	01SEP15	01JAN09	01MAY20	01MAY20
4th	01SEP18	01SEP18	01SEP18	01SEP18	01SEP18
Certain Religious Workers	01SEP18	01SEP18	01SEP18	01SEP18	01SEP18
5th Unreserved (including C5, T5, I5, R5)	C	08SEP15	01APR17	C	C
5th Set Aside: Rural (20%)	C	C	C	C	C
5th Set Aside: High Unemployment (10%)	C	C	C	C	C
5th Set Aside: Infrastructure (2%)	C	C	C	C	C

*Employment Third Preference Other Workers Category: Section 203(e) of the Nicaraguan and Central American Relief Act (NACARA) passed by Congress in November 1997, as amended by Section 1(e) of Pub. L. 105-139, provides that once the Employment Third Preference Other Worker (EW) cut-off date has reached the priority date of the latest EW petition approved prior to November 19, 1997, the 10,000 EW numbers available for a fiscal year are to be reduced by up to 5,000 annually beginning in the following fiscal year. This reduction is to be made for as long as necessary to offset adjustments under the NACARA program. Since the EW final action date reached November 19, 1997 during Fiscal Year 2001, the reduction in the EW annual limit to 5,000 began in Fiscal Year 2002. For Fiscal Year 2023 this reduction will be limited to approximately 150.

A. FINAL ACTION DATES FOR EMPLOYMENT-BASED PREFERENCE CASES

On the chart below, the listing of a date for any class indicates that the class is oversubscribed (see paragraph 1); "C" means current, i.e., numbers are authorized for issuance to all qualified applicants; and "U" means unauthorized, i.e., numbers are not authorized for issuance. (NOTE: Numbers are authorized for issuance only for applicants whose priority date is **earlier** than the final action date listed below.)

Sep 2023 FY23

Employment-based	All Chargeability Areas Except Those Listed	CHINA-mainland born	INDIA	MEXICO	PHILIPPINES
1st	01AUG23	01FEB22	01JAN12	01AUG23	01AUG23
2nd	01JUL22	08JUL19	01JAN11	01JUL22	01JUL22
3rd	01MAY20	01SEP19	01JAN09	01MAY20	01MAY20
Other Workers	01MAY20	01SEP15	01JAN09	01MAY20	01MAY20
4th	01SEP18	01SEP18	01SEP18	01SEP18	01SEP18
Certain Religious Workers	01SEP18	01SEP18	01SEP18	01SEP18	01SEP18
5th Unreserved (including C5, T5, I5, R5)	C	08SEP15	01APR17	C	C
5th Set Aside: Rural (20%)	C	C	C	C	C
5th Set Aside: High Unemployment (10%)	C	C	C	C	C
5th Set Aside: Infrastructure (2%)	C	C	C	C	C

*Employment Third Preference Other Workers Category: Section 203(e) of the Nicaraguan and Central American Relief Act (NACARA) passed by Congress in November 1997, as amended by Section 1(e) of Pub. L. 105–139, provides that once the Employment Third Preference Other Worker (EW) cut-off date has reached the priority date of the latest EW petition approved prior to November 19, 1997, the 10,000 EW numbers available for a fiscal year are to be reduced by up to 5,000 annually beginning in the following fiscal year. This reduction is to be made for as long as necessary to offset adjustments under the NACARA program. Since the EW final action date reached November 19, 1997 during Fiscal Year 2001, the reduction in the EW annual limit to 5,000 began in Fiscal Year 2002. For Fiscal Year 2023 this reduction will be limited to approximately 167.

A. FINAL ACTION DATES FOR EMPLOYMENT-BASED PREFERENCE CASES

On the chart below, the listing of a date for any class indicates that the class is oversubscribed (see paragraph 1); "C" means current, i.e., numbers are authorized for issuance to all qualified applicants; and "U" means unauthorized, i.e., numbers are not authorized for issuance. (NOTE: Numbers are authorized for issuance only for applicants whose priority date is **earlier** than the final action date listed below.)

Oct 2023 FY24

Employment-based	All Chargeability Areas Except Those Listed	CHINA-mainland born	INDIA	MEXICO	PHILIPPINES
1st	C	15FEB22	01JAN17	C	C
2nd	08JUL22	01OCT19	01JAN12	08JUL22	08JUL22
3rd	01DEC21	01JAN20	01MAY12	01DEC21	01DEC21
Other Workers	01AUG20	01JAN16	01MAY12	01AUG20	01MAY20
4th	01JAN19	01JAN19	01JAN19	01JAN19	01JAN19
Certain Religious Workers	U	U	U	U	U
5th Unreserved (including C5, T5, I5, R5)	C	01OCT15	15DEC18	C	C
5th Set Aside: Rural (20%)	C	C	C	C	C
5th Set Aside: High Unemployment (10%)	C	C	C	C	C
5th Set Aside: Infrastructure (2%)	C	C	C	C	C

*Employment Third Preference Other Workers Category: Section 203(e) of the Nicaraguan and Central American Relief Act (NACARA) passed by Congress in November 1997, as amended by Section 1(e) of Pub. L. 105-139, provides that once the Employment Third Preference Other Worker (EW) cut-off date has reached the priority date of the latest EW petition approved prior to November 19, 1997, the 10,000 EW numbers available for a fiscal year are to be reduced by up to 5,000 annually beginning in the following fiscal year. This reduction is to be made for as long as necessary to offset adjustments under the NACARA program. Since the EW final action date reached November 19, 1997 during Fiscal Year 2001, the reduction in the EW annual limit to 5,000 began in Fiscal Year 2002. For Fiscal Year 2024 this reduction will be limited to approximately 150.

A. FINAL ACTION DATES FOR EMPLOYMENT-BASED PREFERENCE CASES

On the chart below, the listing of a date for any class indicates that the class is oversubscribed (see paragraph 1); "C" means current, i.e., numbers are authorized for issuance to all qualified applicants; and "U" means unauthorized, i.e., numbers are not authorized for issuance. (NOTE: Numbers are authorized for issuance only for applicants whose priority date is **earlier** than the final action date listed below.)

Employment-based	All Chargeability Areas Except Those Listed	CHINA-mainland born	INDIA	MEXICO	PHILIPPINES
1st	C	15FEB22	01JAN17	C	C
2nd	15JUL22	01OCT19	01JAN12	15JUL22	15JUL22
3rd	01DEC21	01JAN20	01MAY12	01DEC21	01DEC21
Other Workers	01AUG20	01JAN16	01MAY12	01AUG20	01MAY20
4th	01JAN19	01JAN19	01JAN19	01JAN19	01JAN19
Certain Religious Workers	01JAN19	01JAN19	01JAN19	01JAN19	01JAN19
5th Unreserved (including C5, T5, I5, R5)	C	01OCT15	15DEC18	C	C
5th Set Aside: Rural (20%)	C	C	C	C	C
5th Set Aside: High Unemployment (10%)	C	C	C	C	C
5th Set Aside: Infrastructure (2%)	C	C	C	C	C

Nov 2023 FY24

*Employment Third Preference Other Workers Category: Section 203(e) of the Nicaraguan and Central American Relief Act (NACARA) passed by Congress in November 1997, as amended by Section 1(e) of Pub. L. 105-139, provides that once the Employment Third Preference Other Worker (EW) cut-off date has reached the priority date of the latest EW petition approved prior to November 19, 1997, the 10,000 EW numbers available for a fiscal year are to be reduced by up to 5,000 annually beginning in the following fiscal year. This reduction is to be made for as long as necessary to offset adjustments under the NACARA program. Since the EW final action date reached November 19, 1997 during Fiscal Year 2001, the reduction in the EW annual limit to 5,000 began in Fiscal Year 2002. For Fiscal Year 2024 this reduction will be limited to approximately 150.

A. FINAL ACTION DATES FOR EMPLOYMENT-BASED PREFERENCE CASES

On the chart below, the listing of a date for any class indicates that the class is oversubscribed (see paragraph 1); "C" means current, i.e., numbers are authorized for issuance to all qualified applicants; and "U" means unauthorized, i.e., numbers are not authorized for issuance. (NOTE: Numbers are authorized for issuance only for applicants whose priority date is **earlier** than the final action date listed below.)

Employment-based	All Chargeability Areas Except Those Listed	CHINA-mainland born	INDIA	MEXICO	PHILIPPINES
1st	C	15FEB22	01JAN17	C	C
2nd	15JUL22	22OCT19	01JAN12	15JUL22	15JUL22
3rd	01DEC21	22JAN20	01MAY12	01DEC21	01DEC21
Other Workers	01AUG20	01JAN16	01MAY12	01AUG20	01MAY20
4th	01JAN19	01JAN19	01JAN19	01JAN19	01JAN19
Certain Religious Workers	U	U	U	U	U
5th Unreserved (including C5, T5, I5, R5)	C	01OCT15	15DEC18	C	C
5th Set Aside: Rural (20%)	C	C	C	C	C
5th Set Aside: High Unemployment (10%)	C	C	C	C	C
5th Set Aside: Infrastructure (2%)	C	C	C	C	C

*Employment Third Preference Other Workers Category: Section 203(e) of the Nicaraguan and Central American Relief Act (NACARA) passed by Congress in November 1997, as amended by Section 1(e) of Pub. L. 105-139, provides that once the Employment Third Preference Other Worker (EW) cut-off date has reached the priority date of the latest EW petition approved prior to November 19, 1997, the 10,000 EW numbers available for a fiscal year are to be reduced by up to 5,000 annually beginning in the following fiscal year. This reduction is to be made for as long as necessary to offset adjustments under the NACARA program. Since the EW final action date reached November 19, 1997 during Fiscal Year 2001, the reduction in the EW annual limit to 5,000 began in Fiscal Year 2002. For Fiscal Year 2024 this reduction will be limited to approximately 150.

A. FINAL ACTION DATES FOR EMPLOYMENT-BASED PREFERENCE CASES

On the chart below, the listing of a date for any class indicates that the class is oversubscribed (see paragraph 1); "C" means current, i.e., numbers are authorized for issuance to all qualified applicants; and "U" means unauthorized, i.e., numbers are not authorized for issuance. (NOTE: Numbers are authorized for issuance only for applicants whose priority date is **earlier** than the final action date listed below.)

Jan 2024 FY24

Employment-based	All Chargeability Areas Except Those Listed	CHINA-mainland born	INDIA	MEXICO	PHILIPPINES
1st	C	01JUL22	01SEP20	C	C
2nd	01NOV22	01JAN20	01MAR12	01NOV22	01NOV22
3rd	01AUG22	01SEP20	01JUN12	01AUG22	01AUG22
Other Workers	01SEP20	01JAN17	01JUN12	01SEP20	01MAY20
4th	15MAY19	15MAY19	15MAY19	15MAY19	15MAY19
Certain Religious Workers	15MAY19	15MAY19	15MAY19	15MAY19	15MAY19
5th Unreserved (including C5, T5, I5, R5)	C	08DEC15	01DEC20	C	C
5th Set Aside: Rural (20%)	C	C	C	C	C
5th Set Aside: High Unemployment (10%)	C	C	C	C	C
5th Set Aside: Infrastructure (2%)	C	C	C	C	C

*Employment Third Preference Other Workers Category: Section 203(e) of the Nicaraguan and Central American Relief Act (NACARA) passed by Congress in November 1997, as amended by Section 1(e) of Pub. L. 105-139, provides that once the Employment Third Preference Other Worker (EW) cut-off date has reached the priority date of the latest EW petition approved prior to November 19, 1997, the 10,000 EW numbers available for a fiscal year are to be reduced by up to 5,000 annually beginning in the following fiscal year. This reduction is to be made for as long as necessary to offset adjustments under the NACARA program. Since the EW final action date reached November 19, 1997 during Fiscal Year 2001, the reduction in the EW annual limit to 5,000 began in Fiscal Year 2002. For Fiscal Year 2024 this reduction will be limited to approximately 150.

A. FINAL ACTION DATES FOR EMPLOYMENT-BASED PREFERENCE CASES

On the chart below, the listing of a date for any class indicates that the class is oversubscribed (see paragraph 1); "C" means current, i.e., numbers are authorized for issuance to all qualified applicants; and "U" means unauthorized, i.e., numbers are not authorized for issuance. (NOTE: Numbers are authorized for issuance only for applicants whose priority date is **earlier** than the final action date listed below.)

Feb 2024 FY24

Employment-based	All Chargeability Areas Except Those Listed	CHINA-mainland born	INDIA	MEXICO	PHILIPPINES
1st	C	01JUL22	01SEP20	C	C
2nd	15NOV22	01JAN20	01MAR12	15NOV22	15NOV22
3rd	01SEP22	01SEP20	01JUL12	01SEP22	01SEP22
Other Workers	01SEP20	01JAN17	01JUL12	01SEP20	01MAY20
4th	15MAY19	15MAY19	15MAY19	15MAY19	15MAY19
Certain Religious Workers	15MAY19	15MAY19	15MAY19	15MAY19	15MAY19
5th Unreserved (including C5, T5, I5, R5)	C	15DEC15	01DEC20	C	C
5th Set Aside: Rural (20%)	C	C	C	C	C
5th Set Aside: High Unemployment (10%)	C	C	C	C	C
5th Set Aside: Infrastructure (2%)	C	C	C	C	C

*Employment Third Preference Other Workers Category: Section 203(e) of the Nicaraguan and Central American Relief Act (NACARA) passed by Congress in November 1997, as amended by Section 1(e) of Pub. L. 105-139, provides that once the Employment Third Preference Other Worker (EW) cut-off date has reached the priority date of the latest EW petition approved prior to November 19, 1997, the 10,000 EW numbers available for a fiscal year are to be reduced by up to 5,000 annually beginning in the following fiscal year. This reduction is to be made for as long as necessary to offset adjustments under the NACARA program. Since the EW final action date reached November 19, 1997 during Fiscal Year 2001, the reduction in the EW annual limit to 5,000 began in Fiscal Year 2002. For Fiscal Year 2024 this reduction will be limited to approximately 150.

A. FINAL ACTION DATES FOR EMPLOYMENT-BASED PREFERENCE CASES

On the chart below, the listing of a date for any class indicates that the class is oversubscribed (see paragraph 1); "C" means current, i.e., numbers are authorized for issuance to all qualified applicants; and "U" means unauthorized, i.e., numbers are not authorized for issuance. (NOTE: Numbers are authorized for issuance only for applicants whose priority date is **earlier** than the final action date listed below.)

Mar 2024 FY24

Employment-based	All Chargeability Areas Except Those Listed	CHINA-mainland born	INDIA	MEXICO	PHILIPPINES
1st	C	15JUL22	01OCT20	C	C
2nd	22NOV22	01JAN20	01MAR12	22NOV22	22NOV22
3rd	08SEP22	01SEP20	01JUL12	08SEP22	08SEP22
Other Workers	08SEP20	01JAN17	01JUL12	08SEP20	01MAY20
4th	01DEC19	01DEC19	01DEC19	01DEC19	01DEC19
Certain Religious Workers	01DEC19	01DEC19	01DEC19	01DEC19	01DEC19
5th Unreserved (including C5, T5, I5, R5)	C	15DEC15	01DEC20	C	C
5th Set Aside: Rural (20%)	C	C	C	C	C
5th Set Aside: High Unemployment (10%)	C	C	C	C	C
5th Set Aside: Infrastructure (2%)	C	C	C	C	C

*Employment Third Preference Other Workers Category: Section 203(e) of the Nicaraguan and Central American Relief Act (NACARA) passed by Congress in November 1997, as amended by Section 1(e) of Pub. L. 105-139, provides that once the Employment Third Preference Other Worker (EW) cut-off date has reached the priority date of the latest EW petition approved prior to November 19, 1997, the 10,000 EW numbers available for a fiscal year are to be reduced by up to 5,000 annually beginning in the following fiscal year. This reduction is to be made for as long as necessary to offset adjustments under the NACARA program. Since the EW final action date reached November 19, 1997 during Fiscal Year 2001, the reduction in the EW annual limit to 5,000 began in Fiscal Year 2002. For Fiscal Year 2024 this reduction will be limited to approximately 150.

A. FINAL ACTION DATES FOR EMPLOYMENT-BASED PREFERENCE CASES

On the chart below, the listing of a date for any class indicates that the class is oversubscribed (see paragraph 1); "C" means current, i.e., numbers are authorized for issuance to all qualified applicants; and "U" means unauthorized, i.e., numbers are not authorized for issuance. (NOTE: Numbers are authorized for issuance only for applicants whose priority date is **earlier** than the final action date listed below.)

Apr 2024 FY24

Employment-based	All Chargeability Areas Except Those Listed	CHINA-mainland born	INDIA	MEXICO	PHILIPPINES
1st	C	01SEP22	01MAR21	C	C
2nd	15JAN23	01FEB20	15APR12	15JAN23	15JAN23
3rd	22NOV22	01SEP20	15AUG12	22NOV22	22NOV22
Other Workers	08OCT20	01JAN17	15AUG12	08OCT20	01MAY20
4th	01NOV20	01NOV20	01NOV20	01NOV20	01NOV20
Certain Religious Workers	U	U	U	U	U
5th Unreserved (including C5, T5, I5, R5)	C	15DEC15	01DEC20	C	C
5th Set Aside: Rural (20%)	C	C	C	C	C
5th Set Aside: High Unemployment (10%)	C	C	C	C	C
5th Set Aside: Infrastructure (2%)	C	C	C	C	C

*Employment Third Preference Other Workers Category: Section 203(e) of the Nicaraguan and Central American Relief Act (NACARA) passed by Congress in November 1997, as amended by Section 1(e) of Pub. L. 105-139, provides that once the Employment Third Preference Other Worker (EW) cut-off date has reached the priority date of the latest EW petition approved prior to November 19, 1997, the 10,000 EW numbers available for a fiscal year are to be reduced by up to 5,000 annually beginning in the following fiscal year. This reduction is to be made for as long as necessary to offset adjustments under the NACARA program. Since the EW final action date reached November 19, 1997 during Fiscal Year 2001, the reduction in the EW annual limit to 5,000 began in Fiscal Year 2002. For Fiscal Year 2024 this reduction will be limited to approximately 150.

A. FINAL ACTION DATES FOR EMPLOYMENT-BASED PREFERENCE CASES

On the chart below, the listing of a date for any class indicates that the class is oversubscribed (see paragraph 1); "C" means current, i.e., numbers are authorized for issuance to all qualified applicants; and "U" means unauthorized, i.e., numbers are not authorized for issuance. (NOTE: Numbers are authorized for issuance only for applicants whose priority date is **earlier** than the final action date listed below.)

May 2024 FY24

Employment-based	All Chargeability Areas Except Those Listed	CHINA-mainland born	INDIA	MEXICO	PHILIPPINES
1st	C	01SEP22	01MAR21	C	C
2nd	15JAN23	01FEB20	15APR12	15JAN23	15JAN23
3rd	22NOV22	01SEP20	15AUG12	22NOV22	22NOV22
Other Workers	08OCT20	01JAN17	15AUG12	08OCT20	01MAY20
4th	01NOV20	01NOV20	01NOV20	01NOV20	01NOV20
Certain Religious Workers	01NOV20	01NOV20	01NOV20	01NOV20	01NOV20
5th Unreserved (including C5, T5, I5, R5)	C	15DEC15	01DEC20	C	C
5th Set Aside: Rural (20%)	C	C	C	C	C
5th Set Aside: High Unemployment (10%)	C	C	C	C	C
5th Set Aside: Infrastructure (2%)	C	C	C	C	C

*Employment Third Preference Other Workers Category: Section 203(e) of the Nicaraguan and Central American Relief Act (NACARA) passed by Congress in November 1997, as amended by Section 1(e) of Pub. L. 105-139, provides that once the Employment Third Preference Other Worker (EW) cut-off date has reached the priority date of the latest EW petition approved prior to November 19, 1997, the 10,000 EW numbers available for a fiscal year are to be reduced by up to 5,000 annually beginning in the following fiscal year. This reduction is to be made for as long as necessary to offset adjustments under the NACARA program. Since the EW final action date reached November 19, 1997 during Fiscal Year 2001, the reduction in the EW annual limit to 5,000 began in Fiscal Year 2002. For Fiscal Year 2024 this reduction will be limited to approximately 150.

A. FINAL ACTION DATES FOR EMPLOYMENT-BASED PREFERENCE CASES

On the chart below, the listing of a date for any class indicates that the class is oversubscribed (see paragraph 1); "C" means current, i.e., numbers are authorized for issuance to all qualified applicants; and "U" means unauthorized, i.e., numbers are not authorized for issuance. (NOTE: Numbers are authorized for issuance only for applicants whose priority date is **earlier** than the final action date listed below.)

Employment-based	All Chargeability Areas Except Those Listed	CHINA-mainland born	INDIA	MEXICO	PHILIPPINES
1st	C	01SEP22	01MAR21	C	C
2nd	15JAN23	01FEB20	15APR12	15JAN23	15JAN23
3rd	22NOV22	01SEP20	22AUG12	22NOV22	22NOV22
Other Workers	08OCT20	01JAN17	22AUG12	08OCT20	01MAY20
4th	01NOV20	01NOV20	01NOV20	01NOV20	01NOV20
Certain Religious Workers	01NOV20	01NOV20	01NOV20	01NOV20	01NOV20
5th Unreserved (including C5, T5, I5, R5)	C	15DEC15	01DEC20	C	C
5th Set Aside: Rural (20%)	C	C	C	C	C
5th Set Aside: High Unemployment (10%)	C	C	C	C	C
5th Set Aside: Infrastructure (2%)	C	C	C	C	C

*Employment Third Preference Other Workers Category: Section 203(e) of the Nicaraguan and Central American Relief Act (NACARA) passed by Congress in November 1997, as amended by Section 1(e) of Pub. L. 105-139, provides that once the Employment Third Preference Other Worker (EW) cut-off date has reached the priority date of the latest EW petition approved prior to November 19, 1997, the 10,000 EW numbers available for a fiscal year are to be reduced by up to 5,000 annually beginning in the following fiscal year. This reduction is to be made for as long as necessary to offset adjustments under the NACARA program. Since the EW final action date reached November 19, 1997 during Fiscal Year 2001, the reduction in the EW annual limit to 5,000 began in Fiscal Year 2002. For Fiscal Year 2024 this reduction will be limited to approximately 150.

A. **FINAL ACTION DATES FOR EMPLOYMENT-BASED PREFERENCE CASES**

On the chart below, the listing of a date for any class indicates that the class is oversubscribed (see paragraph 1); "C" means current, i.e., numbers are authorized for issuance to all qualified applicants; and "U" means unauthorized, i.e., numbers are not authorized for issuance. (NOTE: Numbers are authorized for issuance only for applicants whose priority date is **earlier** than the final action date listed below.)

Jul 2024 FY24

Employment-based	All Chargeability Areas Except Those Listed	CHINA-mainland born	INDIA	MEXICO	PHILIPPINES
1st	C	01NOV22	01FEB22	C	C
2nd	15MAR23	01MAR20	15JUN12	15MAR23	15MAR23
3rd	01DEC21	01SEP20	22SEP12	01DEC21	01DEC21
Other Workers	01JAN21	01JAN17	22SEP12	01JAN21	01MAY20
4th	01JAN21	01JAN21	01JAN21	01JAN21	01JAN21
Certain Religious Workers	01JAN21	01JAN21	01JAN21	01JAN21	01JAN21
5th Unreserved (including C5, T5, I5, R5)	C	15DEC15	01DEC20	C	C
5th Set Aside: Rural (20%)	C	C	C	C	C
5th Set Aside: High Unemployment (10%)	C	C	C	C	C
5th Set Aside: Infrastructure (2%)	C	C	C	C	C

*Employment Third Preference Other Workers Category: Section 203(e) of the Nicaraguan and Central American Relief Act (NACARA) passed by Congress in November 1997, as amended by Section 1(e) of Pub. L. 105-139, provides that once the Employment Third Preference Other Worker (EW) cut-off date has reached the priority date of the latest EW petition approved prior to November 19, 1997, the 10,000 EW numbers available for a fiscal year are to be reduced by up to 5,000 annually beginning in the following fiscal year. This reduction is to be made for as long as necessary to offset adjustments under the NACARA program. Since the EW final action date reached November 19, 1997 during Fiscal Year 2001, the reduction in the EW annual limit to 5,000 began in Fiscal Year 2002. For Fiscal Year 2024 this reduction will be limited to approximately 150.

A. FINAL ACTION DATES FOR EMPLOYMENT-BASED PREFERENCE CASES

On the chart below, the listing of a date for any class indicates that the class is oversubscribed (see paragraph 1); "C" means current, i.e., numbers are authorized for issuance to all qualified applicants; and "U" means unauthorized, i.e., numbers are not authorized for issuance. (NOTE: Numbers are authorized for issuance only for applicants whose priority date is **earlier** than the final action date listed below.)

Aug 2024 FY24

Employment-based	All Chargeability Areas Except Those Listed	CHINA-mainland born	INDIA	MEXICO	PHILIPPINES
1st	C	01NOV22	01FEB22	C	C
2nd	15MAR23	01MAR20	15JUL12	15MAR23	15MAR23
3rd	01DEC21	01SEP20	22OCT12	01DEC21	01DEC21
Other Workers	01JAN21	01JAN17	22OCT12	01JAN21	01MAY20
4th	01JAN21	01JAN21	01JAN21	01JAN21	01JAN21
Certain Religious Workers	01JAN21	01JAN21	01JAN21	01JAN21	01JAN21
5th Unreserved (including C5, T5, I5, R5)	C	15DEC15	01DEC20	C	C
5th Set Aside: Rural (20%)	C	C	C	C	C
5th Set Aside: High Unemployment (10%)	C	C	C	C	C
5th Set Aside: Infrastructure (2%)	C	C	C	C	C

*Employment Third Preference Other Workers Category: Section 203(e) of the Nicaraguan and Central American Relief Act (NACARA) passed by Congress in November 1997, as amended by Section 1(e) of Pub. L. 105-139, provides that once the Employment Third Preference Other Worker (EW) cut-off date has reached the priority date of the latest EW petition approved prior to November 19, 1997, the 10,000 EW numbers available for a fiscal year are to be reduced by up to 5,000 annually beginning in the following fiscal year. This reduction is to be made for as long as necessary to offset adjustments under the NACARA program. Since the EW final action date reached November 19, 1997 during Fiscal Year 2001, the reduction in the EW annual limit to 5,000 began in Fiscal Year 2002. For Fiscal Year 2024 this reduction will be limited to approximately 150.

A. FINAL ACTION DATES FOR EMPLOYMENT-BASED PREFERENCE CASES

On the chart below, the listing of a date for any class indicates that the class is oversubscribed (see paragraph 1); "C" means current, i.e., numbers are authorized for issuance to all qualified applicants; and "U" means unauthorized, i.e., numbers are not authorized for issuance. (NOTE: Numbers are authorized for issuance only for applicants whose priority date is **earlier** than the final action date listed below.)

Sep 2024 FY24

Employment-based	All Chargeability Areas Except Those Listed	CHINA-mainland born	INDIA	MEXICO	PHILIPPINES
1st	C	01NOV22	01FEB22	C	C
2nd	15MAR23	01MAR20	15JUL12	15MAR23	15MAR23
3rd	01DEC20	01SEP20	22OCT12	01DEC20	01DEC20
Other Workers	01DEC20	01JAN17	22OCT12	01DEC20	01MAY20
4th	01JAN21	01JAN21	01JAN21	01JAN21	01JAN21
Certain Religious Workers	01JAN21	01JAN21	01JAN21	01JAN21	01JAN21
5th Unreserved (including C5, T5, I5, R5)	C	15DEC15	01DEC20	C	C
5th Set Aside: Rural (20%)	C	C	C	C	C
5th Set Aside: High Unemployment (10%)	C	C	C	C	C
5th Set Aside: Infrastructure (2%)	C	C	C	C	C

*Employment Third Preference Other Workers Category: Section 203(e) of the Nicaraguan and Central American Relief Act (NACARA) passed by Congress in November 1997, as amended by Section 1(e) of Pub. L. 105-139, provides that once the Employment Third Preference Other Worker (EW) cut-off date has reached the priority date of the latest EW petition approved prior to November 19, 1997, the 10,000 EW numbers available for a fiscal year are to be reduced by up to 5,000 annually beginning in the following fiscal year. This reduction is to be made for as long as necessary to offset adjustments under the NACARA program. Since the EW final action date reached November 19, 1997 during Fiscal Year 2001, the reduction in the EW annual limit to 5,000 began in Fiscal Year 2002. For Fiscal Year 2024 this reduction will be limited to 157.

A. FINAL ACTION DATES FOR EMPLOYMENT-BASED PREFERENCE CASES

On the chart below, the listing of a date for any class indicates that the class is oversubscribed (see paragraph 1); "C" means current, i.e., numbers are authorized for issuance to all qualified applicants; and "U" means unauthorized, i.e., numbers are not authorized for issuance. (NOTE: Numbers are authorized for issuance only for applicants whose priority date is **earlier** than the final action date listed below.)

Oct 2024 FY25

Employment-based	All Chargeability Areas Except Those Listed	CHINA-mainland born	INDIA	MEXICO	PHILIPPINES
1st	C	C	08NOV22	01FEB22	C	C
2nd	15MAR23	22MAR20	15JUL12	15MAR23	15MAR23
3rd	15NOV22	01APR20	01NOV12	15NOV22	15NOV22
Other Workers	01DEC20	01JAN17	01NOV12	01DEC20	01DEC20
4th	01JAN21	01JAN21	01JAN21	01JAN21	01JAN21
Certain Religious Workers	U	U	U	U	U
5th Unreserved (including C5, T5, I5, R5)	C	15JUL16	01JAN22	C	C
5th Set Aside: Rural (20%)	C	C	C	C	C
5th Set Aside: High Unemployment (10%)	C	C	C	C	C
5th Set Aside: Infrastructure (2%)	C	C	C	C	C

*Employment Third Preference Other Workers Category: Section 203(e) of the Nicaraguan and Central American Relief Act (NACARA) passed by Congress in November 1997, as amended by Section 1(e) of Pub. L. 105-139, provides that once the Employment Third Preference Other Worker (EW) cut-off date has reached the priority date of the latest EW petition approved prior to November 19, 1997, the 10,000 EW numbers available for a fiscal year are to be reduced by up to 5,000 annually beginning in the following fiscal year. This reduction is to be made for as long as necessary to offset adjustments under the NACARA program. Since the EW final action date reached November 19, 1997 during Fiscal Year 2001, the reduction in the EW annual limit to 5,000 began in Fiscal Year 2002. For Fiscal Year 2025 this reduction will be limited to approximately 150.

A. FINAL ACTION DATES FOR EMPLOYMENT-BASED PREFERENCE CASES

On the chart below, the listing of a date for any class indicates that the class is oversubscribed (see paragraph 1); "C" means current, i.e., numbers are authorized for issuance to all qualified applicants; and "U" means unauthorized, i.e., numbers are not authorized for issuance. (NOTE: Numbers are authorized for issuance only for applicants whose priority date is **earlier** than the final action date listed below.)

Nov 2024 FY25

Employment-based	All Chargeability Areas Except Those Listed	CHINA-mainland born	INDIA	MEXICO	PHILIPPINES
1st	C	08NOV22	01FEB22	C	C
2nd	15MAR23	22MAR20	15JUL12	15MAR23	15MAR23
3rd	15NOV22	01APR20	01NOV12	15NOV22	15NOV22
Other Workers	01DEC20	01JAN17	01NOV12	01DEC20	01DEC20
4th	01JAN21	01JAN21	01JAN21	01JAN21	01JAN21
Certain Religious Workers	01JAN21	01JAN21	01JAN21	01JAN21	01JAN21
5th Unreserved (including C5, T5, I5, R5)	C	15JUL16	01JAN22	C	C
5th Set Aside: Rural (20%)	C	C	C	C	C
5th Set Aside: High Unemployment (10%)	C	C	C	C	C
5th Set Aside: Infrastructure (2%)	C	C	C	C	C

*Employment Third Preference Other Workers Category: Section 203(e) of the Nicaraguan and Central American Relief Act (NACARA) passed by Congress in November 1997, as amended by Section 1(e) of Pub. L. 105-139, provides that once the Employment Third Preference Other Worker (EW) cut-off date has reached the priority date of the latest EW petition approved prior to November 19, 1997, the 10,000 EW numbers available for a fiscal year are to be reduced by up to 5,000 annually beginning in the following fiscal year. This reduction is to be made for as long as necessary to offset adjustments under the NACARA program. Since the EW final action date reached November 19, 1997 during Fiscal Year 2001, the reduction in the EW annual limit to 5,000 began in Fiscal Year 2002. For Fiscal Year 2025 this reduction will be limited to approximately 150.

A. FINAL ACTION DATES FOR EMPLOYMENT-BASED PREFERENCE CASES

On the chart below, the listing of a date for any class indicates that the class is oversubscribed (see paragraph 1); "C" means current, i.e., numbers are authorized for issuance to all qualified applicants; and "U" means unauthorized, i.e., numbers are not authorized for issuance. (NOTE: Numbers are authorized for issuance only for applicants whose priority date is **earlier** than the final action date listed below.)

Dec 2024 FY25

Employment-based	All Chargeability Areas Except Those Listed	CHINA-mainland born	INDIA	MEXICO	PHILIPPINES
1st	C	08NOV22	01FEB22	C	C
2nd	15MAR23	22MAR20	01AUG12	15MAR23	15MAR23
3rd	15NOV22	01APR20	08NOV12	15NOV22	15NOV22
Other Workers	01DEC20	01JAN17	08NOV12	01DEC20	01DEC20
4th	01JAN21	01JAN21	01JAN21	01JAN21	01JAN21
Certain Religious Workers	01JAN21	01JAN21	01JAN21	01JAN21	01JAN21
5th Unreserved (including C5, T5, I5, R5)	C	15JUL16	01JAN22	C	C
5th Set Aside: Rural (20%)	C	C	C	C	C
5th Set Aside: High Unemployment (10%)	C	C	C	C	C
5th Set Aside: Infrastructure (2%)	C	C	C	C	C

*Employment Third Preference Other Workers Category: Section 203(e) of the Nicaraguan and Central American Relief Act (NACARA) passed by Congress in November 1997, as amended by Section 1(e) of Pub. L. 105-139, provides that once the Employment Third Preference Other Worker (EW) cut-off date has reached the priority date of the latest EW petition approved prior to November 19, 1997, the 10,000 EW numbers available for a fiscal year are to be reduced by up to 5,000 annually beginning in the following fiscal year. This reduction is to be made for as long as necessary to offset adjustments under the NACARA program. Since the EW final action date reached November 19, 1997 during Fiscal Year 2001, the reduction in the EW annual limit to 5,000 began in Fiscal Year 2002. For Fiscal Year 2025 this reduction will be limited to approximately 150.

Works Cited

"The Visa Bulletin." U.S. Department of State, U.S. Department of State travel.state.gov/content/travel/en/legal/visa-law0/visa-bulletin.html. Accessed 19 Nov. 2024.

www.ingramcontent.com/pod-product-compliance
Lightning Source LLC
LaVergne TN
LVHW022325080426
835508LV00013BA/1327